SHEDDING SKINS

AMERICAN INDIAN STUDIES SERIES
Gordon Henry, *Series Editor*

Editorial Board

Kimberly Blaeser	Heid Erdrich	Winona LaDuke
Joseph Bruchac	Matthew Fletcher	Patrick LeBeau
George Cornell	P. Jane Hafen	John Petoskey

- *Shedding Skins: Four Sioux Poets*
  Edited by Adrian C. Louis | 978-0-87013-823-2

- *Writing Home: Indigenous Narratives of Resistance*
  Michael D. Wilson | 978-0-87013-818-8

SHEDDING SKINS

FOUR SIOUX POETS

Trevino L. Brings Plenty
Steve Pacheco
Joel Waters
Luke Warm Water

Edited by Adrian C. Louis

MICHIGAN STATE UNIVERSITY PRESS ▪ EAST LANSING

∞ The paper used in this publication meets the minimum requirements of ANSI/NISO Z39.48-1992 (R 1997) (Permanence of Paper).

 Michigan State University Press
East Lansing, Michigan 48823-5245

Printed and bound in the United States of America.

17 16 15 14 13 12 11 10 09 08   1 2 3 4 5 6 7 8 9 10

LIBRARY OF CONGRESS CATALOGING-IN-PUBLICATION DATA
Shedding skins : four Sioux poets / Trevino L. Brings Plenty, Steve
Pacheco, Joel Waters, Luke Warm Water ; edited by Adrian C. Louis.
p. cm. — (American Indian studies series)
ISBN 978-0-87013-823-2 (pbk. : alk. paper)
1. American poetry—Indian authors. 2. Dakota Indians—Poetry. 3. Indians
of North America—Poetry. I. Brings Plenty, Trevino L. II. Pacheco, Steve.
III. Waters, Joel. IV. Warm Water, Luke. V. Louis, Adrian C.
PS591.I55S54 2008
811'.540808975243
2007038515

Cover design by Heather Truelove Aiston
Book design by Sharp Des!gns, Inc.
Cover art is "The Gate" and is used courtesy of the artist, Wang Ping
Photo of Luke Warm Water on page 90 is © 2005 Linda Spizzirri and
used courtesy of the photographer

green Michigan State University Press is a member of the Green
press Press Initiative and is committed to developing and en-
INITIATIVE couraging ecologically responsible publishing practices. For more infor-
mation about the Green Press Initiative and the use of recycled paper in
book publishing, please visit *www.greenpressinitiative.org*.

Visit Michigan State University Press on the World Wide Web at
www.msupress.msu.edu

Contents

Joel Waters

Introduction

Adrian C. Louis

The End of the Trail Is a Beginning of the Trail

I wasn't some troll caged by
the gravity of a dank bridge,
but I was compressed under
the arc of a whitening sky
when I heard them whisper.

"We like him somewhat.
He knows to fart precisely
the moment the saddle rises."

The dumb bastards did not
know I always rode bareback
& spoke their secret tongue.
I'd loitered in their mother's
womb, had suckled her books
in her oak-leathered rooms.

My haggard horse hung low
his head, his neck my pillow
& his back was my bed.
"Fine," they said. "Sleep
deep & bring us a dream."

So we did & we were running
in shimmering delight, delirious

in the strength of our youth.
Our fertile flanks foamed in
the sunlight *&* our hooves did
not skitter when we hit rocks.
Past the stones *&* onto sand,
we whirled, dashed around
& over rabbit brush *&* sage
& heard voices that seemed to
come from the whitening sky.
"You bring us a dream. You
& not that goddamned nag."

They did not know the horse
& I were one blood, one bone.
Such purchase was beyond
their deep pockets so we ran
& ran like a son of a bitch
until the sky reddened *&*
we stalled in a sentence
of sweat *&* self-love.

Sometimes I wonder which carriers of Native culture are the most
important. That culture itself is not a static commodity, that it is
a constantly evolving creature is often not factored into the public
equation. Some people think those Indians who adopt a public
persona—the artists, the writers, the actors, the historians, the
educators, etc.—provide the greater sustenance of tribal ways. Others
say the grassroots people, the less formally educated singers, medicine
people, story tellers, and community activists are more important.

In this anthology of four Sioux poets, I think you will find a
combination of the two. And while I know that the term "Sioux" is
rapidly falling out of favor with those it is applied to, I used the
word because of the mixture of tribes involved. Two of the writers,
Joel Waters and Kurt Schweigman (who chooses to write under the

name Luke Warm Water) are Oglala Lakota. Trevino Brings Plenty is Minneconjou Lakota, and Steve Pacheco is Mdewakanton Dakota. And they all are male. Perhaps someone soon will do a compilation of women poets of the Great Sioux Nation.

On the surface, the subject matter of the poems may seem extremely similar, but with a careful reading each individual poet becomes his own planet, his own galaxy. While each evokes stinging traces of the hardships of reservation life on the northern plains, each paints his own portrait of what it means to be a Sioux Indian in these times and survive. Joel Waters and Steve Pacheco tend to have more of an academic influence in their work. Warm Water and Brings Plenty have cut their teeth in the field of Slam and performance poetry. Waters is finishing up his degree at the University of South Dakota. Pacheco completed his MFA in creative writing at the University of Minnesota and now teaches high school. Brings Plenty now lives in Portland, Oregon, where he is a musician in addition to being a writer. Warm Water works in the American Indian public health field and recently moved from Rapid City, South Dakota, to California.

The poems in *Shedding Skins* cut to the bone with their honesty, and we live in an age where honesty is an orphan. But these four poets offer brilliant and insightful portrayals of Native pain, hope, joy, and overall, survival. In the flickering neon of these poems, you can smell the commodities cooking; you can hear the old ones singing. Many of the poems in this collection make the leap from the common/mundane to the truly visionary, and this allows the reader a rare taste of epiphany. These four young Skins frequently take a local starting point and transform it into a universal truth. Let them take you into their worlds. Finally, I need to thank my friend the poet Wang Ping for the cover photo of the medicine wheel which is not a medicine wheel at all but art work on an ancient gate in China. Peace out.

TREVINO L. BRINGS PLENTY

Here We Go Again

I sat in a chair
in Lucy's new apartment.
Another lady was there
who I never met.

She introduced herself and said
her name was Alicia.
She sat at my feet facing me.
She had blue eyes, auburn hair, fake 'n bake skin.
She asked if I was Native American.
I said, "Yes."
"Native Americans are so cool," she said.
"They are very spiritual.
They are in touch with the earth,
 and, oh my god, there is the Great Spirit.
You have a beautiful culture."
"It's not all mine," I said.
"Native Americans have so much wisdom,"
 she said and leaned closer to me.
"Do you know any sacred stories?
 Can you tell me a story?"

"Okay," I said.
"This one took place in old times.
There was a lone cavalry soldier.
He was stationed at an abandoned
fort in South Dakota.
There were Lakotas not far off.
The Lakotas watched this man
 and wondered at his strangeness.
They saw him cleaning the fort.
They thought he was crazy to be alone.

Then they saw him trying to communicate
with a wolf that had white front paws."

Alicia interrupted me and said,
"That is the storyline for
Dances with Wolves."
"Yes it is," I said.
Then Alicia stood behind me
and started to run her fingers
through my hair.
"It's unfair," she said,
"Indian men have such beautiful hair.
It's so dark and thick and soft.
You are a beautiful man."
"Thanks," I said, "But you know
I have more of that beautiful hair
around my cock."
Alicia quickly pulled her hand away.
"You're disgusting!" she screamed.
"Maybe so," I said, "But your ideas
of me are just as repulsive."
Then Alicia sat on my lap and kissed my cheek.
She stood and left the apartment.

"There you go, Trevino," Lucy said,
"You have a great way with the ladies."
"Yeah, I know," I said, "The crazy ones
come to me like flies to dog shit."

Ghost Shirt Litany

I wear her dead father's shirts
which are heavier than muslin shrouds.
He is in the ground
from an overdose
and I sit on green grass
thinking which kind of
bugs are crawling through
his bones.

I wear these shirts
every day.
They are worn out.
Some with cigarette holes,
some with puke stains,
some too warm for summer.

All these shirts
in my closet,
all these nights
I pass out on the couch,
and wake before the starlings.

I am caged in these clothes,
in this red world,
in this destruction,
in these ghost shirts.

How to Be an Indian Male in the Early 21st Century

You must be birthed from an Indian mother.
She must be in her teens.
She must come from an alcoholic lineage.
And you must say this is so.

You will never meet your father.
You will grow uncertain about your manhood.
You will be angry.
This must be so.

You will sit in a cafeteria,
greasy fries and cheeseburger before you.
You will know all these people
are all different ideas.
All these people will never leave.

A bearded white man sitting twenty feet away
will look you over.
He will wonder at your cheekbones,
your long hair in a ponytail,
your dark brown skin.
He will want to ask what tribe you are.

He will feel sorry for you
and your people's history.
He will imagine you half naked
like what he saw on TV last night
and what he has read in his large
Western novel collection.

He will hate you
because you don't fit his model.

You will see this bearded white man.
You know he is watching you.
You will imagine him in the same
period clothes as he was with you.

You will feel sorry for him.
You will sip your water in a clear plastic cup.
You will imagine the bearded white man
wearing buckled shoes, tan stockings, knickers, puffy shirt,
vest, topcoat, and a large-brim hat.

You will wonder when his glory days
ever began. You know he smells foul.
The white man has maybe bathed once a year.
This was the strange custom of white people.
You will start to mimic the way he is eating
and sound out the strange nuances of his language.
It will anger you when you look around
the cafeteria and see mostly white people.

The white woman five feet away wearing a yellow dress
and dipping bread into her soup will see you.
She will want to take home a dark man.
She will hate you
because her husband is white.
Her life is easy,
it has to be.
She has two white children.
She will leave this family.
She will use you.
She will break your heart.

But she doesn't do this to hurt you;
she does this to leave her unhappy marriage.

You see this white woman in a yellow dress.
Her wedding ring is very expensive.
You imagine her wearing a low-cut red dress.
You imagine her leaving her family.
She must be unhappy with her life.
You know she is watching you.
You know you must end her marriage.
You will be in your late thirties.
The anger you had all your life
will eat you alive.
You will drink heavily.
You will not care
when your mother calls long-distance.
You will let your answering machine pick her up.

You will die from a fatal injury.
This must be so, but not until diabetes sets
in your body and most of your sight is gone.
You will be a dead Indian male underground.
All the noise you had in your head
will finally be silenced.

This could be one end to your story.

To Rid the Egg

It wasn't long ago
third world reservations
destroyed hope
in the newest generation's possibilities.

In the '70s
my mother was damn lucky
she was not
sterilized by IHS butchers.

My mother,
a brown woman,
birthing U.S. enemies;

brown children
that grew up
in urban California.

Here I am
years later
waking to new information
on the death of my genes,
death of my land.

Making it out
of the doubt
I had in my facial structure

I say now it was luck,
but really it was
survival. empty space

My mother saving
her grace in the children
she nourished
while piecing together
who she was
in a manifest destiny world.

Mothers are creators
of what we are;
part history,
part failure,
part discovery,
part resolution,
all fire.

Indian women
birth those who will
demolish
this monster
that controls all.

This machine
created
to liquidate
brown people.

In the U.S.
my mother survived
sterilization empty space
by empty space
secret legislature, empty space.

The Question

We lived in San Jose, CA
on welfare, commodities, WIC.
Found broken toys and ill-fitted clothes
at a Goodwill drop-off.
I attended mostly all white schools.
I hated my coarse black hair,
my large cheekbones, brown skin,
and very Indian sounding name.
We lived off of the city,
ate $1.50 tacos with diet soda,
and on weekends with family,
partied until early morning crying fits.
My mother's mother drank herself to death.
My mother's father chose homelessness
and pushed a shopping cart.
My uncles would sit in a back room
cooking up heroin or hubba rocks.
Indians in a city, that's what we were,
powwows in college gyms,
moving every year into different motels
or cheap rooming houses by railroad tracks
kept warm by open oven heat.
TV, public transit, white families
every year giving us used board games, clothes, food
while me and my siblings hid in a closet,
watching them wanting to help an Indian family
not struggle.
To be Indian is not to be a savior for white people.
To be Indian in a city is not tragic.
And now you ask me where I am from.
I understand your question,

but will answer it with, "Next question."
Alive in America is all we are.
Let's leave it at that.

No Eyes

1.

My grandfather had his eyes stolen.
He said they were
in a Smithsonian Museum.
The last image he saw
was a blond-haired woman
bending over him.
He was newly back from Japan,
he was still wearing his WWII uniform.
He said it wasn't a good thing,
but he was sadly satisfied his eyes
were set next to his grandparents' bones.

2.

My grandfather was a brakeman
in his late teens.
When he lost his left pinkie finger,
he quit and joined the army.
"There were a lot of Indians
in the army," he said,
"We were seen as American heroes
when we wore our uniforms."
He said,
"Know this, grandson,
the people were not all warriors.
My cousin was a painter and storyteller,
my brother was a fisherman,
my sister tamed horses,
everyone ate food, breathed air, drank water.
This is the family lineage."
My grandfather rolled a cigarette.
He was wearing sunglasses.

It was evening just before supper.
"Every man wants to huff and puff
their warriorness," he said,
"But the real work is peace."

To Find the Indian Wisdom

She is a lingerie model.
She has orgasms for money.
I am Native American, an Indian, to be precise.
Sex for money, this keeps our rent and food going.
She thought because I am Indian,
I come with extra knowledge/wisdom.
She wants me to be the earth she walks,
this is not how it is.
I am a man who is not earth.
I am a man who is in need as anybody else.
I accept her work and that is all.
To her, I am well-grounded,
not that I have feelings, in fact
there is no feeling when the job is sex.
I am dead and I am dead.
I am a man, but really another consumer.
We all fool ourselves with love.
I hate her for what she does,
but she pays the rent and keeps me alive.
Besides, what's the point of living anyways,
to be hollow in what I believe and want day and night?
NO. KEEP SELF ALIVE ONLY.
THERE IS NOTHING ELSE.
I am an idea, she is a woman,
both don't work when money is exchanged.   ı
After our last fight,
I kicked her out the door
and threw five dollars at her.
She was worth her full pay
and I gave it to her.
She is gone and I am alive.
What more can you ask.

Park Sandwich

I sleep in a park across from a church,
the San Francisco sun on my face.
I vomit on the grass.
I load my bags over my shoulder.
I don't need anything else.
My feet hurt from
walking around town,
and a good drink will be great.
The church is handing out
a PB&J sandwich, chips, a can of soda.
I eat this down,
drink the soda with
an Indian woman with wild hair.
She smells like she is packed
full of cum and shit.
She asks if I want some company,
she will do me good.
I think hard about this,
and say no.
My cock is sore
from too much masturbation
with cheap lotion,
so much so that my right palm
is just as chapped as my cock.
She says she is Spokane Indian,
her name is Charmaine Elixer.
I say to her I'm visiting from Portland, OR.
She pulls from her pack
some sweet grass and
gives it to me.
I light it and cover
my face with smoke and throw it.

"What you do that for?" she asks.
"I don't need all that shit," I say.
She kicks my shin
and picks up the burning strand
and covers my feet and body with smoke.
"Brother, stay strong," she says,
"I can tell you got something
good about you.
I love you."
"You don't know me."
"How did you feel when I said it? Good, huh."
"Good ain't great and great ain't good."
"You are a smart fucker, enit."
"I know some things."
"Stay strong, brother,
we are Indian and
have inherited the earth.
Our lost white brothers and
sisters have destroyed us and built
this shitty city."
"It was bound to happen
sooner or later."
"Stay strong.
Take care."
She walks out of the park
and into the void of the city.
I feel holy and American.
I take a bottle from my pack,
take a pull,
stand and walk into the same void.

Building Rooms to Sell Dreams

I sit on brick steps
after work with my homeless
friend, Red.
He said he woke this morning
to rain hitting his face.
He was dreaming of his mother
beating him with a plastic
slot car racetrack.
Each hit across his body
was the love he hadn't known,
the truest sense of safety lashing him.
He dreamed of his uncle
holding him down, face buried
in the thick, carpeted floor.
Naked and cold,
the lights on in the living room,
the TV showing rap videos,
his uncle said he would kill him
if he told anyone.
Each thrust Red received
was someone taking an interest
in his life, it was lovemaking
to an Indian boy and Red
closed his eyes from then on.

I smoke a cigarette and
take a pull on my beer.
"Those are only dreams, Red," I said.
He said, "I don't dream anymore,
I only remember."

Part Gravel, Part Water, All Indian

It's not by accident
I live in a city.

It was calculated:
a bloodline of misery,

a nonwhite skin,
a tongue not made for English,

years to germinate genocidal loss.
I live to wait as anybody else

not for handouts,
but hand-me-down lives:

work boots, white T-shirts, blue jeans.
I am the Other of this

American Other masked in common clothes.
My homeland is occupied by debt.

My language is not in my dreams.
My heart is ripped to shreds.

My lungs burn with fire/smoke.
My body is diseased by civilization.

My mind is a nomadic madness.
I live where concrete sterilizes life.

Life Money

"Fuck you!" the young, white guy yelled
into the hot mid-afternoon air
while walking past me.
I was smoking a cigarette
at the entrance of a natural food store
across the street from a pawn shop.

What the hell is this?
I thought, blowing out smoke
and making a fist.
I looked down at my only weapon;
an acoustic guitar in a hard-shell case.

The white guy was with
two white girls and another white guy.
They were crossing the street
when a mumbled, "Fuck you"
in response came from around the corner.
Then the white guy yelled again,
"'Fuck you?' Took you long enough!"
and continued to walk away, laughing.

I knew it was a homeless drunk that mumbled.
I didn't want it to be,
but when I looked around the corner,
two Indian guys,
my age, sat on the sidewalk.
They were bumming change,
wasted out of their minds.
They were cursing
at the white gang.

I pulled hard at my smoke
and felt like kicking the shit
out of every white male I saw.
I pulled hard again and
walked to the Indian guys.
"Hey, where you from?" one of them asked.
"I'm a Lakota from South Dakota," I answered.
"Hey, brother," the other guy said,
"I know you don't like seeing us like this."
"Shit, man," I said, "You are still a skin."
I dug deep into my pockets and gave them
my change. I rolled them two cigarettes each.
"Thanks," they said in unison.
I saw it in their eyes,
those Indian eyes in love with drinking.
"Take care," I said and walked
to the pawn shop across the street.
I had to make rent this month.
I live paycheck to paycheck.
I could easily be homeless.
My grandfather was homeless.
Shit, I am in a city
miles from my homeland.
Damn near homeless.

I love to drink and
I've seen it in my eyes
many times, many nights.
A dangerous love
made mad of this world.
And an unbearably white thing
yelling at me,
"FUCK YOU!"

Lakota Language Lesson with Benjamin

I sit at the kitchen table
with my grandfather.
We are learning the Lakota language.
We listen to a cassette recording
he made three years ago.

We sound out the strange words together.
We say the words for
all my relations, good,
woman, horse, cat, dog, home.

All those drinking years he had—
I remember them all.
His marriage, years as a chief
in the Marines, no-good alcoholic children,
grandchildren's birthdays, his youngest brother
who drowned, the remaining brother who died
two years ago, his ex-wife who died last year.
My grandfather can't recall any of these.

A brain blood clot pressed down
and crushed his memory.
A year after surgery he has regained
his motor functions and speech.

My grandfather and I take a break
from our language lesson.
I make him a ham and cheese
sandwich on 12-grain wheat bread.
I place it on a plate
with a handful of baked potato chips.
I set the plate in front of him

and he says, "Thank you, sir."
I open a can of diet cola and
pour it into a plastic cup with ice.
I drink from the can and set
the cup next to his plate.
He says, "Thank you, sir."
"*Lala*," I say, "We are doing good, enit."
He says, "*Wast´e.*"

It was dusk when my grandfather
and his two younger brothers
were drinking near the Cheyenne River.
The youngest wanted to swim across
the river. My two grandfathers
drove in a pickup truck over a bridge
and parked on the other side.
My grandfathers watched their youngest
brother sink in the middle of the river.
They couldn't do anything about it.

"*Lala*," I say. "I think we are doing good, enit."
My grandfather smiles and says, "*Wast´e,*"
and takes a bite from his sandwich and eats
a couple of chips. He asks for a straw,
I get one, and place it in his cup.

In the mornings I dress my grandfather in
blue jeans and a western shirt. He slips on
his white tube socks and brown cowboy boots.
He stands before a mirror and combs thinning hair.
"Phoebe," I say to him. "That was your wife's name."
"Phoebe," he says, "that's a funny name."

"Major and Abraham," I say to him.
"Those were your brothers."
"Yes," he says, "Major and Abraham."

Before his surgery my grandfather talked at me
in the Lakota language, point blank.
When I was younger, I asked him at a powwow
if the Lakota drum group sang any words.
My grandfather laughed at this and said, "Yes, *Takoja*."
Three years ago I remember my grandfather sitting
at the kitchen table with a tape recorder in front of him.
He said he was making these tapes for his grandchildren.
When I'm away from my grandfather he asks my wife
where that nice man went, not remembering that
I am his grandson. My wife says, "He went to school."
"When is he coming back?" he asks.
"Soon," she says. She says, "Soon."

I press play on the cassette player after my grandfather
finishes his meal. We sound out more Lakota words.
As we sit at the table, he says,
"My voice sounds funny on that machine."
I say, "The language sounds funny, enit."
He says, "The words feel like home."
I say to him, "I think we are doing good, *Lala*."
My grandfather looks at me and says,
"*Wast´e, Takoja*. We are doing good."

Meals

Mine is a red owl
asleep in the day
and hunting in the night.

I keep it well fed
lest it claw my lungs,
tear my kidneys.

Most of the time
it is calm,
beautifully perched
in my chest.

But sometimes, it
turns its body,
opens its wings,
and flies into the dark.

Then I am alone
looking for purpose,
finding the sadness
of my hands
touching my face,
combing my hair,
tending old wounds.

When the owl returns,
I keep it awake
out of anger

until it throws up
its meal.
I choke on the loves

it has hunted,
who were once
all of my loves.

Dead Whistle

She walks around the parking lot
whistling for someone.
Here I sit watching her,
wondering if I should
answer her call.
That is one way to find
something, whistle,
but the dead don't answer
whistles in the day,
and be wary if you call
at night, they will come.
They come, I guess, like most
after living flesh,
a conversation, or
company.
She walks away and
I don't follow.
I sit and wait
for the next one.

Crazy Horse Nightmares

In my dreams,
I ride a red horse.
This beast is fear.
It is my friend,
father, confessor,
my will to go
deeper into the night.
I am headed home.
I am alive and chased
by Crazy Horse.
I feel his arrows hit
my body.
Each one is made
from those I had
let down,
those who loved me,
those who wondered
at my anger.

Who is my death bringer?
The one who loves my body?
The one whose desire
is to take part
in my soul?
Have you made
these arrows to fling
at this huge piece of meat,
these bones,
this skull?

Here I am
living the history

that brought me
to the now
in the work I do.

We all want to be warriors,
but if war is all the time,
there are no winners.
In this, how do I measure
the small triumphs
against this self-doubt?
Where is the beauty
I am to walk?
Half of my life is
not in my control.
Half of my life
is destroyed by
Crazy Horse nightmares.

I wake to count the glories
in one hand,
and in the other palm
hold the happiness
that can kill me,
that can set me free,
that I am needing to swallow,
and finally be safe
among the shadows
that circle my days
and cover me at dusk.

I am an urban Indian
in a city of broken people.

I am the one who killed Crazy Horse
in every Indian
on any street corner,
office desk, or barstool.
I killed those who made a hero
out of a warrior.

She Is Now a Poem

We meet for a few beers.
I let her read one of my newest verses.
She has all my books,
but this one is a new piece.
She reads it and tears up
at my contemplation of night.
We talk about
antidepressants, suicide attempts,
hospital visits, and shrinks.
"If we had children," she says,
"They would look like us
black hair, brown eyes, cheekbones."
Then we are in my single bed.
She darts her tongue in and out of my mouth.
I have to pull her hair to slow her down.
I teach her to kiss.
I suck on her huge tits,
her areolas are shaped like faint stars.
She leaves her panties on.
She won't let me slide in.
"It's a mess down there," she says,
"I'm on my period."
She says, "It's a good thing
we don't do it, I want children."
She moans when we kiss and
I poke at her black panties.
"If you can't be a poet," I say,
"then be the poem."
"I know," she says.
We kiss at the door.
She leaves, walks into that
great, lonely night I wrote about.

I relieve myself in bed alone
thinking about her tits,
her moans,
what she would've felt like,
and my disdain for children.

It Is Called a Chow Line

I see them every morning
waiting for breakfast
in a line along a building
wrapping around the city block.
Homeless men and women
smoking cigarettes,
nipping at bottles,
wiping rain from brow.
They squat or stand,
then the line moves
into the soup kitchen.
The meal is free.
It is warm inside
as they sit at tables,
swiping S.O.S. with
a flaky biscuit,
and blow before
sipping on their hot coffee.
During the meal
there is laughter,
a small prayer is answered.
They stay as long as they can
until they walk the streets
and sleep somewhere out of the rain.

STEVE PACHECO

History

Cousin, how useless now
are the dirt road days
when we whirled roundhouse
kicks at one another with our bare feet,

and how we listened to our fathers
kindle the fire water in the kitchen
gives us January memories

of times we spent in the gravel pit
playing war with plastic Army men
only tells half the history
of the little lives we razed.

Your first winter home
snowfall arrived early.
The multihued hills of the rez
turned the same color brown
as your camouflage fatigues.
I thought it was coincidence.
Maybe the snow flourished
to welcome you like a kindred spirit.
Maybe, *tahansi,* it was our time
for history to surround us.

City Elegy for a Nameless Skin

And indeed if it be the Design of Providence to extirpate these savages
in order to make room for the Cultivators of the Earth, it seems not
improbable that Rum may be the appointed Means.

—Benjamin Franklin

Stagger-stepping down
the infamous Franklin Ave.
with a Marlboro dangling from my lips.
It's 1:30 A.M. and I'm going nowhere
Cold night in a cold city
where gangs and pimps are kings
of dirty streets and hundred dollar hustles.
By a bridge, an old Indian man,
high on wine asks me for some spare change.
I flip him a five and look at his weathered face
holding forty years of relocated pain.
Remnants of gold paint speckled
across his mouth from huffing fumes
to either escape the pain, or end it,
I don't know which. In his face,
I see a young Indian boy.
In his face I see that this city
is no place for an Indian.

Uncle

I've seen the greatest punch ever thrown.
A sharp short left hook to the jaw
of Kenny "The Cobra" Jones.

Dear Uncle's swift hands of stone
left us stunned, in awe.
I've seen the greatest punch ever thrown.

Indians fight back. Uncle John
slurs, quivers, but retells what we saw
when he punched Kenny "The Cobra" Jones.

After endless years of staggering home
whiskey bottles hidden in the basement below
I've seen the greatest punch ever thrown.

He sits on the front porch alone
staring, his mind recalling how
he punched Kenny "The Cobra" Jones.

The leather gloves still glisten
in a box beneath old clothes even now.
I saw the greatest punch ever thrown
when Uncle John beat Kenny "The Cobra" Jones.

Indian Country

They sang the smoky night away. They sang songs of heartbreak and cattle and booze. They sang about open prairies and ex's living in Texas. They sang about cheating hearts. They sang Merle, Johnny, Hank, Patsy, and George. They wore beaded belt buckles and black cowboy hats with feathers. We tried on their black leather vests and ribbon shirts. We put on their boots and tripped on the carpet. They sang over 8-tracks, over our TV, out the windows, into the country rez night.

Bottles, ashtrays, cans on the table. Poker chips, a deck of cards, some spare change. Like that the morning came. A bike ride to the store for worms and minnows. The afternoon smell of fish frying in the kitchen, masking the smells from the night before.

Veteran's Day

for Wallace J. Smith Jr., 82nd Airborne

I still think of that morning when I tried to imitate a crow and fell on my face. Their loud caws outside the barred windows of your garden-level apartment made me get up and hop on one leg. We just returned from the Veteran's Day powwow in Sisseton and you'd been home less than a year, working security at the casino.

You showed me pictures of young men on tanks. You pulled out your beret and said how you missed the winters. Before the blizzard began we sipped on coffee and talked about god, liquor, and our fathers.

Lonesome Night

I grew up under the swaying hips of Elvis. I watched his legs move side to side like the pendulum on a grandfather clock, hitting each beat of *Blue Suede Shoes.* Father, in his oil scented work clothes, strutted around the house to *Go Cat Go,* posed in vintage Elvis, and all the children loved him.

I once peeked out my bedroom door to see him sing *Are You Lonesome Tonight?* He slow danced in the kitchen with an imaginary woman. Within weeks he cut his hair like Elvis and left for the cities.

I come back to that lonesome night every time I think of my father. And like the children of the house, I too want to remember him like I remember Elvis—young, handsome, and unaffected.

Rocks

*for M.B. and the incarcerated Indians of the Lino Lakes
Correctional Facility circa 1999.*

You called a week earlier
saying the brothers were low
on sage and rocks for the sweat.
I still had "Black Beauty"
that rusty '78 pickup
abandoned behind the shed.
I loaded the bed with rocks
from the river, large round ones
that turn aglow from fire,
ingrained along the steep banks
where we first witnessed
the shrill cry of a rabbit
clutched in the beak
of a red-tail hawk.

Spirits, you said
the river's known to do that.
You took tobacco and sprinkled it
on the ground before we ran
from the thunderheads creeping
over the tree line.

Brother, when you come home
we'll go back to the boat landing,
throw rocks high in the air
anticipating the sound
of rock / hitting / water.

And if we should hear
the rabbit's death,

or the sky turns black overhead,
this time we'll stay to watch
like we should've done
the time of year when
chokecherries ripen.

Waiting for the Barbarians

My mother and the rest of the kids from the rez walked to school every day, and when they got to the bottom of the hill the kids from town waited so they could throw things from behind the trees, pat their hands over their mouths, and run to the schoolyard. Once, when my mother was hit with a stick, she ran home to tell her brother. That night he gathered up his friends and went down to the bottom of the hill before sunrise to wait for the kids from town to show. When the rez boys heard the kids approaching, they hid behind the trees. When the kids reached the grove, the rez boys grabbed them by their shirts and brought them to the train trestle where they showed the kids from town some rope and said they were going to tie them to the tracks. My uncle's friend Freddy, the crazy one, held one kid over the edge by his ankles, dangling him over the river. After the rez boys made the kids from town run to the schoolyard crying, they walked back up the hill and passed by my mother and the rest of the kids from the rez walking to school, and they didn't exchange a word.

Sugar Bowl

after Etheridge Knight

I.

There's a running joke within my family about diabetes. It goes like this. When you meet someone and they ask you what type of Indian you are, you answer by either saying Type I or Type II. The reality is nearly everyone in my family has the disease. My mother. My father. All my grandparents, before they died. Three of five aunts (two dead). Three of four uncles (three dead). Each person spent the latter part of their life with a whole new vocabulary of insulin, blood sugar level, and, to me, the scariest word I remember as a child, dialysis.

II.

I watched my Uncle Steve disappear in front of my adolescent eyes. It started with his toes, then half of his foot, then all of his foot. Next he lost a finger, and then a couple more . . . When Uncle Steve died, he was in a wheelchair, missing half a leg and six fingers.

III.

The old saying is that diabetes skips a generation, but with my family it didn't even skip siblings. In later years, after I went to college, I read numerous books that discuss the epidemic of diabetes among American Indian communities. It was there I learned about the food of my parents' youth—government commodities—food that the government sends to reservations. Growing up, commodities were always in our shelves, but I never knew what they contained. High in fat. Preservatives. Salt. All of which lead to things like obesity, alcoholism, and of course, diabetes. From these texts I learned the scariest word of my adult life, genocide.

IV.

Each year at Christmastime my mother puts out two bowls of candy—sugar and sugarless. Sometimes I catch her sneaking from the sugar bowl and remind her to only take one. She returns the favor to me when I reach for the salt to put on anything.

V.

He dealt with the disease the same way our family dealt with most things, through humor. On Sundays our family gathered to watch football. An all-conference running back himself in high school, Uncle Steve looked forward to these events, and like everybody else, he was a huge Minnesota Vikings fan. When the Vikings would score, instead of saying, "gimme five," he would say, "Alright nephew! gimme three." And I would stick out my thumb, pinky, and index finger to touch his as the people around us whooped and hollered.

VI.

During the harsh prairie winters the pipes under our house would freeze. We boiled snow so that we had something to cook with and something to eat. We drank syrupy canned grape juice. We ate powdered milk and powdered eggs. And bacon. On more than one occasion, I remember eating bacon for breakfast and dinner. To us children, the burnt bits were a treat like rock candy. When the grease hardened in the pan, we spread it over Wonder Bread.

Our Life

I looked for my father in littered streets of the cities. He told me stories of the hardcore joints he loved—bikers, ex-cons, Indians trying to get home. I searched the names from memory. *Moby Dick's, The Commodore, Mr. Art's,* and *The Abyss.*

I sat next to an Indian man, tall and skinny, wearing a red sweatshirt with the faded word in white, Haskell.

He wanted to know my story (I wanted to know his). I told him my name and he said he knew my father from boarding school days at Marty Mission. We talked over the jukebox about common kin and forgotten friends.

It was our life that night. A loner and a bastard. At closing we shook hands and headed down separate paths in the moonless blue night that is America.

Arrival Song

I am a man of so many homecomings
　　　　　　　　—Pablo Neruda

July. Catfish. Minnesota River.
Stars shine and shoot across
the black template of another prairie night.
Water kisses granite, and retreats.
Boulders lodged in mud
mark the years we leave,
only to come back.

This is the time of berries.
This is the year of open arms.
Embrace the trestles and all
its rotting wood. The old
wagon bridge. The cold springs.
Birch Coulee. Sage budding
on the hillside.

Embrace it all. The tracks
we walk along to come home.
Our return to summer stories
told at the gatherings.

But Tonight I Praise It

The ceaseless prairie winds fended mosquitoes while sparrows struggled to land on the increasingly bare branches. Autumn. The time of year when green hills of the river turn into a dead brown, and the geese fly from the same direction as the wind.

I heard them this evening. It sounded like war whoops, but when I looked to the low clouds: nothing. Just *wakiya* putting on a light show down the horizon. I picked up the small gifts the wind had left at my feet, and thanked it for its resilient grace.

Prairie Prayer

A quiet night except for the usual
music of crickets and frogs croaking.
Everything depends on the river.
Mist covers the valley and the harvest moon
drapes September air. Tonight we notice
deer tracks engraved in soft dirt
along the cottonwoods, we listen
to leaves rustle in the faithful wind.
Born on the banks, this is our home.
Granite fields and rock quarries
carry stories into winter.
The cragged voice of the bluffs remind
us that faces need not be carved in stone.

The Lower Sioux Rez: Three Scenes

I.

I feel I owe something to the blue jays for their loyalty.
February hints at snow, and tricks
cardinals into an early spring-red.
But the blue jays hold their color, and govern
the shrubs behind my house like senators.

II.

The coyote, impossibly scrawny with knots
of orange fur on its legs, paces
on the icy river. Large clumps of snow
drop from cedars and pines. Startled,
she sprints down the open path
unable to scatter to the comfort of trees,
without the ability to run on the steep blue banks.

III.

When the prairie winter folds away like a blanket
legions of frogs return from the river.
In late autumn, they make their odyssey through mud,
covering roads, resting in sloughs.
Their long legs, suspended in air, glimmer
in the cars' headlights.

The frogs come back after *the melt*.
Heavy. Stomachs hard from swallowing stones.

Wacipi

I.

People from everywhere have come
to the Lower Sioux hill to dance and sing
long after the triumphant stars shine

over oaks and pines. The drum echoes
and we know it can be heard
for miles and miles. And the laughter

can be heard for miles and miles
while children run, couples dance,
and small fires smolder.

II.

The rain calms the dust
and the sun dries wet grass
Across the river, a rainbow

arches within the valley's touch.
The food line long with stories,
chatter, and hand shakes.

III.

Have you ever heard the drum beat
and the thunder's bellow fill summer
nights when the river whispers

and the leaves dance before
rain begins to tap the tents
of campers hiding

because they too notice
the absence of emerald
fireflies pulsing by the creek?

Homeland

The lampshade turned stain-yellow
from Pall Malls. Uncle always
smoked non-filter. Past bedtime
I hid behind the recliner
listening to stories about train rides
from Rocky Boy, Montana.

Blended together: Tobacco smoke
wood smoke, and sage.

At the kitchen table he taught
how to play poker and gin rummy.
He showed me how to shuffle and bridge.
We wagered candy canes
and anted salted peanuts.
He cracked the shells for me
until his fingertips grew raw.

Her Belly

Brown and immense her belly
sits in front of her, guides her.

Her belly is round
and highlights her beauty

her legs, her breasts, her mind.
At night she craves ketchup,

oranges, and milk.
I say her belly could be

the moon as I kiss it.
Sometimes I gently rub

her belly in a steady rhythm.
Sometimes I cup it

in my hand feeling for a beat.
I draw circles with my finger

around her oversized belly button.
Most of all, I love to play music

to it softly: the drum.
I want the little one to hear,

feel the drum inside.
I want us all to feel the drum inside.

Star Quilt

The flower patterns faced outside
so the lavender border
framed the window. The eagle's
wings outstretched to the tips
of the star, and her tail fanned
out to the bottom like a winter horizon.

At the giveaway
last summer
you said
the blanket
would keep me
warm in the months
ahead.

With the emergence of winter
winds I took the quilt down
and wrapped myself in its
soft, thick, layers.
The eagle hugged my back
while the star shrouded my body
on the cold wood floor.
Come time for spring and I remember
you, your frail bones, the hours spent
weaving a story with your hands.
And like I learned from the women
of the family:

I looked
for one
crooked
stitch.

On the Anniversary of Her Wake

for Rosie Cloud

I saw her reflection
between the ashen clouds
in the dappled light at dawn.
She wore whirling colors
of red and yellow.

I knew her dance.
She danced among the clouds
from the west as they gathered
to smudge this thirsty land
and tame the smothering dust.

First of the Month

Casino lights and cornfields.
One-armed bandits and one-eyed
jacks lure farmers in flannel
and mesh hats to spend
government pay on jackpot dreams.
The paved road sprawls across the rez
reaching redneck towns where boys
play tag in pickups with CB's.

On the rez roads, dogs
on hunt for food stalk ditches,
the pack scatters when
a couple approaches their path.
The gravel leads to the fire pit.
Tonight, the bass music thumps
from SUVs where skins sit,
waiting for new stories to be told.

Eden Prairie, Minnesota

the hitchhiker points west
with his thumb while he walks
down the freeway. in one hand
he keeps the book wrapped in silk,
neat and convenient. his weathered
face rough like the snake skin
boots he wears for character.

across the apple orchard
past the lush valley, into the prairie
he walks like a giant with purpose.

he walks down the freeway
to the edge of the earth
or the end of america
whichever comes first.

Brothers

I.

We left the reservation early Friday morning to make our way to
Santee, Nebraska. It was our first trip together since Waylon returned
home from the Army where he spent four years jumping out of
airplanes—one of which he did a tour in Iraq in Desert Storm. The
previous night's rain left the ground soft and the air thick. Waylon
waited outside while I was getting our bags. Through the living room
window I watched as he drew lines in the mud with the tips of his shoe.
I never felt more close to my brother than that late August morning.

II.

Cornfields and bean fields. The land farmers somehow thought
tamable. We drove west by southwest down county highways. I stared
out the window at the endless fields of black dirt and it reminded me
of our childhood. We would play outside on the dirt roads with little
plastic figures of green army men. We set them up in strategic places
and shot them down with rubber bands. Because I am five years
younger than my brother, I hardly won. Except for the times, I know
now, he let me.

We stopped in Sioux Falls at a Perkins to get some coffee and
something to eat. Outside the restaurant, there was a huge American
flag. The way it flapped in the constant prairie wind was as constant
as a drum. I pointed to the enormity of it. Waylon nodded. He then
turned to me and said, "That flag is big enough to make outfits for all
the dancers in the world."

III.

As we continued south we listened to the radio and talked about the
past four years. The music was mostly old rock and country because
that's the only choice South Dakota gives you. *"I'm burnin' I'm burnin'*

I'm burnin' for you." I turned it up and said, "You know, this song's all about a guy who catches the clap."

Waylon chuckled and said, "Remember when uncle Mark told us about the time he was in the Philippines, and he saw a dude pass out after taking a piss?"

"Yeah," I said, "because of the pain."

We looked at one another for a brief second and started to laugh. This is how our trip went. We exchanged stories while the land so familiar to us gave way to wheat fields and their crimson colors.

After we arrived in Santee, we visited our cousin's house. Our Aunt Fran knew we were coming so she made space for us to sleep. I could tell Waylon was content. We came here a lot as kids—spent a good portion of our summers here. On this return trip we went to the powwow all day and at night played spades back at Aunt Fran's.

Love Poem

We drove to the VA hospital
where they cut off the remainder
of your toeless foot.

On the way home, we took
the back roads, hoping
to shine a deer

for venison to eat
with the commodity stew
simmering on the stove.

JOEL WATERS

Devil's Playground

I have found myself
Backsliding again.
Back, back, back,
Into the tragic of my kind.
Into the burdens of my stereotypes.
As rednecks in the Midwest
Look at me like I'm an animal at a zoo.
Monkey see, so monkey do.
And what will I do?
When the role they want for me
Is right for the coloring of my skin.
See the red devil?
See that he is the cause of his own sin?
And these labels
They can gnash at you
Make you uneasy.
Make you dizzy.
Like the bullying
Of all your holy
Merry-go-rounds.
Give us sanctity,
Except for the browns.
And we still go swinging
Back and forth
On the history of our beginnings,
And who really owns mother earth.
And the school teachers
The Darwinians
Say it's all about natural selection.
And me and my kind
Are still somehow two shades away
From evolution.

And so you will find us swinging
In the jungle gyms of your mind.
After all this country did its best
To cause the end of my kind.
But see, saw,
Forget it all.
As America expects us all
To play nice with one another.
But in the devil's playground
There are angels,
And there are the unfortunate others.

The Outhouse

The outhouse
Still stands
Behind my grandma's house.
As a reminder of where I come from
Of where I've been.
And that it was not so long ago
That we used to use it
The way the government used us.
No flush! No flush!
It still stands there
Piling up.
Like a reminder
That my family in Pine Ridge
Still uses one.
I'm tired of people asking
Where I come from.
I am a Native American.
But that's not all there is
To me, me, me!
I just want to flush
The toilet!
So I don't have to keep smelling
My poverty.
On the potty
—The potty.
So I party
And I have a good time
Getting wasted.
So I don't have to think of the waste
That is coming out of me,
That is becoming me.
I just want to write good poetry!

But I tear the words
Right off of the
Roll of the role
That I played as a student.
And I ball up those
Words like toilet paper
And I use the world
To wipe my ass.
Because let's face it
Everyone can have a toilet bowl mouth.
And no matter how many times
Flushed or hushed
It's still the same shit swirling about.
But it doesn't matter
Right now!
Because that outhouse is still
Behind my grandma's house.
And I just can't flush
These words these thoughts
Of what I am and what I am not.
And does it define who I am
And what I am anyway
Is just another poet
-Who rephrases, rewrites, reverts,
Verse after verse
Of recycled shit!
And damn it!
I just wish,
I could flush this.

Picking Potatoes

My mother used to pick potatoes
and other vegetables
Along with her dad.
She grew up like that.
She grew as big as she could in a shack.
Next to a huge farmhouse
where there were plenty of rooms
to store the dreams
that were pulled from her
Like weeds.

And then came seventeen
in the mid-seventies.
She had to harvest her sins
She had to bring another life in.
In a time of her great depression,
In a time of an Indian famine.

My older brother
would sit with her
for five minutes at a time
in the field.
Being planted row after row
As mother picked the potatoes.
It's no wonder he never stays long
Anywhere he goes.

His roots don't grow
His roots don't show.
He has put on a covering
Of gangster talk
—Black slang.

Often times he's Mexican
Because he can't
Settle for being just Indian.

And there are many eyes
That look out to the rest of this root-covering world
And we are all guilty of wanting to be another color
Even I used to pray to my pagan god
That I didn't look like my dark-skinned brothers.

The Linoleum Heart

I used to walk barefoot
On the linoleum.
The sticky beer stuck to me
Like men's stuff sticks.
There's a kind of dirtiness
One can get used to.
I know what lies
In beer cans.
I used to collect them
When I was a kid.
Until that night
A man knocked down my pyramid.
I know what lies
In the gazes of drunk men.
I've collected them,
I collect them.

I remember playing
With toy cars.
I used to crash them,
On the linoleum.
The way they crashed him
—My dad
Who was just an outline.
There was nothing anyone could fill in.
Not one crayon.
I knew how to draw mom
But how did I draw you, dad?
I drew others instead.

I used to lie on those older boys
The way ink lies on paper.

I could never understand it.
Maybe it was a metaphor?
Maybe I was just a good whore?
Daddy,
They never told me different.
But I never saw myself
As innocent.
(Like the children of the flesh,
I was born into it.)

I'd lie on the floor
Tracing my future
Chalk line, outline.
—A BODY!
That was never mine.
Until Gestapo boots stomped in.
I was always in fear
Waiting for a final solution.
It was in my blood
—The red paint that got splattered.
And whether I'm lying,
Sitting, or standing.
I find myself in the same old patterns.

On the linoleum,
(A permanent mark)
I am still trying to figure out
—Who I really am.

Wannabe

I used to be able to walk
downtown pine ridge
anytime I wanted
but now I can't even go a block
without some dumb young cock
flashing like a siren
the affiliation he's representing.
Even children have that
hardcore attitude.
And I think "better black than white?"
But either way it does me no good.
Because I know how quickly
things can become ghetto.
As we bust out our windows
and spray paint our walls.
Names emblazoned to show
who has the most scars.
In a culture barely preserved
saran-wrapped, gangster-rapped
while the rest of America
sits and watches
in the spoils of her wars.
It's so easy to become hardcore.
Especially when there is no one
around to hug you and love you
and to say "I'm proud of you,
I believe in you."
It will never matter how in
I wannabe,
Or if what I say is un-American.
I will never put anything
before the importance

of my own skin.
And if it's a choice between black or white
then I'd rather fill my own color in.
Because my family fought hard
and even though they've all fallen
—I'm going to climb out of their beer can coffins.
I'm going to rise from their cigarette ashes,
and make them feel proud again.

Spirits Underneath an Artificial Blue Sky

The boards in the house are loose.
Some are rotting away,
Others have been peeled back.
The black mold
Has filled their chests.
There is no breathing room
But we still live here.

The walls have been
Cracked like smiles
By angry fists and clumsy
Kid hands.
I have written on these walls
An unfinished epitaph.

Stains mark the walls
Like liver spots.
Some are chipped and showing
The true color underneath.
I hate the color.
It is too blue,
As we sleep underneath
Our artificial sky.

No one cleans anymore.
The holes have taken over.
So often we disappear.
—No obligations.
We cover them with rugs
And hideous couches.
Forgetting the things underneath.

We still hold this house together.
We manage to keep the doors locked.
And use the antique dresser
With only so many handles
To hold on to.
These wounds we ignore.
Plug up with tissue,
Hide behind posters.
And we are okay
As long as the white world
Does not peek in.
Because we have been naked
In our savagery
For far too long.

It would be better
If we still lived in teepees.
There are only two holes,
—One on the top
In which we can escape
Into the stars like smoke.
Instead of falling
Through the ones
That are all around our souls.
Making us condemned.
Unfit to live in.

Rez Cars Crash

Seems like all my life
Has been just bits and pieces
Of junk cars, Rez cars
—Loud and exploding
As they pass me by.
Like some bad nightmare
I have to open my eyes.
And everyone I know
Just gives a part of themselves.
A junkyard of living
And then they die
Without me truly knowing them.

Seems like every time
I try to fix up my life
And make it shine
I break down,
And I end up
Hiding inside
My family's house.
Where my dreams rust
And I cover it with lies.

I ignore the problems.
And they become like those
Junk cars
Ditched in the river.
And like them
I am halfway submerged
In the murky water
Of this world's tired womb.
Abort

Breech
And divert.
This contract
That I have made
With god?
The creator? The spirit world?
I am done
Thumbing
Down that highway to heaven
That has claimed so many Indians.

I am just shattered glass
By the side of the road.
And I just want to pop
All egos.
Because no Indian can suffer
More than me.
I am the epitome
Of the tragic Indian
With a backseat
—Back trunk
Full of baggage.
And my therapist
Has tried to break open the lock.
And I myself have used
So many wire hangers
Trying to scratch
At the afterbirth.
Because mom
Never wanted me,
Because dad
Never claimed me.

I am a fetus.
Exposed
And ready to crash.
And Jesus
Everyone on the rez
Is ready to crash.
Implode and explode.
Let our deaths be as violent
As our births.
And maybe when we hit
Head on
We can knock through
The misconception
That we are going
To the white mans' heaven.
Lord, God, Tunkasila (grandfather),
I am tired of stalling
And co-dependently
Waiting for a ride.
I just want to drive
I just want to drive
And then dive into the ditch, and die!

Into the Turtle's Cracks

Into the cracks of the turtle's back I go
feeling weary and old.
I am tired of always surfacing.
Up to my neck in the memories
That drown me.
Let this ground give away
From underneath me.
For the turtle
—She has stood for far too long.

Because my mother,
She was gone like that.
And now there is no footing.
It became easy
To hold on to anyone that came along.
But every home that I had
Began to crack.
Too many beds
For just one back.
So I turned away
From the one night stands
But I am always quick to snap.
Because my mother
—She was cruel like that.

I wandered through many cities
Trying to find stability,
But like the turtle's shell
I am stuck
In the grid
of the city streets
and the country roads.

No matter where I go
I cannot find an edge
but the razors.

So I cut my way home
because mother
had the same veins.
It's in my blood.
The directions.
But no one sees
that I am on my way.
So I tuck my scarred wrists
into my cuffs
and I hide my legs.

I was so young
when I started,
just like she was
when she let me go.
I was always on my own.
Carried too long
on my ancestors' backs.
I just want to slip
into the cracks
because she
was unknown,
unknown like that.
So when mother earth
opens up to me,
I will finally be
. . . at home.

Cherry

Cherry, cherry
—That's what they called me.
Ever since
The blood was made to flow.
Like the time that boy hit me
And made it come out of my nose.
He wanted me
To be weak like a girl.

They used to call me cherry.
Because one day
Someone dressed me up
Like a little doll.
I stood four feet tall,
But still it was a long fall
As they knocked me
To the floor.
They were sickened by me.
As I did a twirl
For them, for them.
It was always for them
—The ones who lost their
Innocence at the stem.

And I was green
At first
And then red
—Blood blooming,
Because I wouldn't
Do what they said.

Cherry
Before I reached
The age of maturity.
Because one night
I met a man,
And was he sweet like family?
Or just another stranger with candy?
I cannot tell,
I do not remember
Such choke cherry things.

But we shared
A bed that night,
And he unwrapped us
Like a tampon.
Just me and him
With only a blanket on.
And I could go on
But I just as well
Would like to stop there.

As a child
I wasn't very tough.
They used to call me cherry
Because faggot
Was a word
That just wasn't enough.

The Cigarette Burns

The cigarette burns
Branded me
Like a fat little
Brown cow
—As dumb as the bell
tied around me.
I must've walked
In loud chunks.
Because HE heard
Every time I left the farm.
Then it was always
Back into the red barn.
As red as my eyes were
When he wrestled me
To the ground.
How the rope burned,
Poking me
Like stitches.
While the other little
Piggies looked on
—Them bitches!
I will never forgive them
For just getting
Cut off at their hogs feet.
While he butchered the rest of me.

But not before leaving
The angry marks
His signature was all over me.
So if the white ranchers
Ever found me
Hiding in their pastures

They'd take me back to him
For sure.
I never minded
Standing in my own feces.
I never minded
Him kicking the shit
Out of my back.
It's just all the scars
That remained after that.

So many cigarette hole-burned
Circles.
Connect the dots
One, two, three,
The image is his
And never me.
And every year
Dragged to the redneck rodeos.
I never had any other place
To go.
When they broke the cattle
I always thought next
It would be my turn.
I have faced it many times
—the cock piece,
Saddle horn,
Stinging spurs.
I always wanted to be a him
But I was always her
—That bitch who left me
To die there.

Soon, soon
A new brand
Will be at home on me.
As I welcome the burn
Of an eminent cancer,
or HIV.
Because even now
I mark myself.
I make my own hell.
But it's not the same burn,
The scars are not as real
As your signature.

 Luke Warm Water

Art of Huffing Paint

All our friends are dead,
Or they're dying,
And our laughter only turns into crying,
It's death-defying.
    —from the Hoodoo Gurus song *Death Defying*

When the green lizard is gone
while you're on the wrong planet
whom silver and gold are your best friends
where train tracks run behind Safeway
Mills Drug Store and Don Margo's Liquor store
near the viaduct from which that sign
proudly proclaimed
North Rapid, A Great Place
circa 1970s Rapid City, South Dakota

Pass out drainage tunnels or
in thickets on abandoned lots
empty Wonder Bread bags
of modern day warrior dreams unfulfilled

Riding my orange Schwinn banana seat bicycle
with the cool black racing stripe fenders
innocence of summer break days
grades take new meaning when
uphill peddling with only one gear
coasting down all too familiar
cracked pavement streets
gravel alleys soaked with black oil
dirt walking paths
keeping my distance
from those unfortunate misplaced

spirited warrior ghosts
my fear stronger than compassion

Maneuvering my bike between
        broken wine bottles
        pot holes
        big rocks
avoiding wipeouts
like a slalom downhill skier
going
for the bronze medal

In turn peddling takes on new meaning
when there are no more food stamps to sell
items stolen or fished out of dumpsters
from Safeway and Mills Drug Store
and a parking lot resale
not enough change for a jug
from Don Margo's Liquor store
so go find that hidden in the weeds
spray paint can again

I had witnessed
too many brown faces with
silver and gold stained lips
not yet comprehending at that young age
this could have been my future

Blip Blip

Sound wave shaped
dagger blade
through the chest
no vital organs hit
as heart is being
digested in guts
exactly
shaped
like a rope

No more
blip blip
on your
radar screen
not like I had
DCA to PDX
not even a
blip blip
for you
in Okie heartland

Most of your
adult life
in the South Dakota
State Penn.
blip blip
bad ass Indian
original gangster
of Rapid City

That
check cashing

payday loans
discount cigarette store
wooden Indian pose
with the bandana
prison tattoos
between
the knuckles
with the 40 oz. beer
wino paper bag
closely hugging
cheap bottle
in a manic clutch
hands sharing
steering wheel
road blurry
as paint brushes
chase
into corners
of dead end
North Rapid
neighborhoods
     no right turn
     for the Red man

Your world
only knew
prison and
our side of town
blip blip
no more
as heartbeat

finds its last
final
violent
thump

In those
final moments
of your fate
I seriously doubt
you reminisce
as kids
sharing our bikes
riding on
Lemmon St.
or
grade school
recess
where no one
could beat you
at shooting marbles
I swear you could hit
a boulder marble
dead on
from 30 ft. away
before
shooting meant
for you;
firearm pistolas
fire arms from
boot'n it needles
blip blip

wash'n it all down
with shots of
fire liquor breath

I wonder
what
must
have
been
in your
thoughts

Just before
you
hung
yourself

Chief Bigfoot Death Pose and the Pawn Shop Receipt

Kit was glad to leave South Dakota behind and cursed its name. He said that if the Communists ever dropped the atomic bomb, he wished they'd put it right in the middle of Rapid City.

> —Sissy Spacek's character Holly Sargis, from the movie *Badlands* (1973)

Cradled in snow
frozen generations
Lakota kids crying
in the backseat
of a rusted nest
one-eyed Chevy
like baby birds
mouths open
end of civilization
on the ice bone wind
fast forward
beyond hangovers
splintered mixed bloods
pretending to be ghosts
while
shopping mall medicine men
medicine women
purchasing the herbs
tinctures of ointments
at health food stores
sporting ponytails
braided so perfect
fixing up the sure-fire
remedy
to get into the souls
of a mid-life crisis
America
curing themselves
along the way

Cradled in snow
frozen fast food wrappers
the new generation fed
parked in front of Kmart
wind whipping
clear plastic bag
is answer
to question of
shattered drivers side
window

Cradled in snow
thick "bucky" Rez accent
tongue that never truly graced
once beautiful language
plastic beads, cloth, silk
diligently intertwined
for a ribbon shirt
of the red bandana protest
1970 something on the "Knee"
awaits the pawn shop
next to Kmart
in 100 years
this ribbon shirt will sit proud
in the Smithsonian
as the Little Big Horn war shirts
sit today

Cradled in snow
frozen tears
church on top of
burial ground

bird on tombstone
from Rapid City tourism
flying due south by
southwest
celebrates
rape of a mountain
four great white grandfathers
then rape of another mountain
some Polish sculptor's
vision of
the greatest Lakota warrior
Tasunke Witko (Crazy Horse)
who never had
his image
trapped
inside a glass photography plate

Cradled in snow
Chief Big Foot's death photo
carved in my mind
as the sound
of the pawn shop
cash register
eats and pukes money
uniformed cashier
writes earnestly
on a small notepad
soldier of sales
he stops and asks for
my signature
which I give then receive
cash loan

he initials the paper
tears it off
he keeps the original
mine is a copy

I am then handed
my newest treaty

Indian Health Service Clinic

Martha Vineyard Livingston
from the East Coast
new resident medical student
seeing patients at a South Dakota Reservation clinic

Martha examined an elder Lakota man
she noticed he was missing all his toes on one foot
Martha asked him what had happened

Old Lakota man responded
with a straight stoic face
"The Bureau of Indian Affairs cut my toes off
one
by
one
because I wouldn't sell my land
so I sold
before they got to the other foot"

"Oh my God!"
Martha believed this
immediately left the exam room
to tell the clinic doctor
what he said
this elderly man needed legal help
he was being extorted

The clinic doctor laughed and laughed
at Martha Vineyard Livingston
the east coast medical student
telling her

that he had his toes removed
from complications of diabetes

This is an example
of not understanding
Indian humor

Welfare Bliss

It happens the first of every month
reminiscent the days
of food stamps turned into cheap wine
months become years
and move with indifference
with a fistful of welfare check money
she put the bad medicine on you
after sundown
and did it with a breath wink
hiccup exclamation
that's how she works
inhaling breath with rage
and expelling it without reason
hiccup again
with the smell of stale beer
and cheap cigarettes on her breath
she is either going to hug and kiss you
or tear you a new asshole
possibly both at some point tonight
either way she'll be feeding you
fried egg sandwiches
in the hangover morning
that's how it works
one Budweiser pitcher at a time

Martin, South Dakota Needed a Martini Waitress

Feelings of loneliness surrounded 3 A.M.

Outside the motel room I listened
to a semitruck
jake break
on nearby Highway 18

Time forgets tribulation
of an Indian Reservation border town

Thoughts turn
to the downtown Martin, South Dakota
greasy spoon café I had dinner at
smile and welcoming phrase
from the white waitress
another Rez Injun customer
did she feel prejudice and greed?
another Rez Injun stranger
did she feel my eyes upon her flirting skirt?
she was young and blonde beautiful
I had shut my eyes for a moment
envisioning sex with her and the patterns
our blonde and black hair would make
on the white pillow case
in my motel room

I ordered another drink and said nothing

Thoughts turn to the silence of sleep

Ishi's Hiding Place

Yahi tribal land
a long way from the streets of San Francisco
no use to go back
only spirits inhabit the land

What was your name Ishi?
your people's custom forbade you to say it
so you were called "man" in Yahi
so anthropologists and newspapers
knew what to call you

One of the few of your tribe who survived
the Three Knolls Massacre
how fitting forty-some years later
in 1911 you appeared near Oroville, California
you willingly emerged to a group of butchers
at a nearby slaughter house corral

What was your name Ishi?
touted the last "wild" Indian
carted off to the University of California in Berkeley
nursed back to health to be studied
under house arrest of the city
and the new civilization
employed as a janitor
in the San Francisco Museum of Anthropology

In 1916 dying of tuberculosis
a death mask prepared in your closing breaths
to be photographed and displayed
while your brain shipped to the Smithsonian

the rest of you cremated
to a San Francisco cemetery

What was you name Ishi?
it was for you to keep alone
your only hiding place
to keep us with a great mystery
but one thing was for certain
after your final breath
no Indian could ever go back

John Wayne's Bullet

Tunkasila (Grandfather)
John Wayne and his like
shot us

Wounded we are recovering
removing the bullets:
>   racism, genocide
>   booze, heroin
>   Big Macs, cable television
>   and so on . . .

Nursing our torn flesh
filling the holes with good medicine
the circle of life
and the seven sacred rights

Gun powder from their dud cartridges
to cauterize our wounds

Building common sense
out of their spent metal casings

Keeping their extracted iron bullets
from our wounds
to construct an impervious *tipi* (lodge)
around our culture

Grandfather
John Wayne's followers are still shooting
with their hammer of greed cocked ready
with their chamber of oppression filled full

with their itchy ignorance finger on the trigger
with their barrel of assimilation aiming down on us

Grandfather
we won't steal John Wayne's gun away
that would make us
just like him
So we are saving gun powder
from their dud cartridges
to cauterize our wounds
searching for their spent casings
from the urban city back alleys
to the Reservation prairies
keeping their extracted iron bullets
from our wounds
to build the new sacred lodge

Tunkasila (Grandfather)
we will soon have saved enough
from American society's nothing

To finally protect our grandchildren
from John Wayne's bullet

Pizza Poem

Are you hungry for pizza?
my Uncle Verlin was 40 years my senior
when questioned about his ethnicity
he would respond
Mostly Sioux Indin'
part German and when
it comes to the drink
full-blooded Irishmn'

Uncle Verlin lived to be an old man
raised on a ranch
on a South Dakota Reservation
by my grandparents
Uncle Verlin was a true cowboy Indian
living out his life
like the songs
Hank Williams Sr. and Woody Guthrie
lamented about
drifting, drinking
leaving a trail
of a half dozen pissed off ex-wives
children claimed and unclaimed
along the path of his life

One night Uncle Verlin and I
polished off a fifth of whiskey
hungry, we decided on pizza
he had seen TV commercials
for Pizza Hut
and wanted to eat at one
for the first time

Upon our arrival
a teenaged white boy asked us
from behind the counter
what we wanted to order
The biggest pizza you have with a lot of extra cheese
Uncle Verlin said
the white kid asked what he wanted
for toppings
Uncle Verlin said
Tiny little white men
the kid behind the counter looked bewildered
asking "What?"
Tiny tiny little white men on my pizza
"Uh sir
we don't have that topping
do you want a different topping?"
NO! I want only tiny tiny little white men on my pizza
the white boy behind the counter
now looked shit scared
after that Uncle Verlin
and I lost it
we laughed and laughed
all the way home
carrying our pizza
with Italian sausage topping

After all
Columbus was Italian
we thought it the next best choice
for a pizza topping

The Jesus of Pine Ridge

The Jesus of the Pine Ridge Indian Reservation
in South Dakota
was raised speaking Lakota
until he was five years old
until he was sent to the Catholic boarding school
on the Rez
where the nuns washed
his native language out of him
every time he was caught speaking Lakota
and they washed in English
with white bar soap

When he was a young teenager
he had the same recurring dream
of nuns crucifying him
atop an old wooden telephone pole
with No.2 lead pencils
driven through his palms and feet
wire notebook binder stretched and wrapped
around his head like a crown of thorns
pages of Big Chief notepad paper fastened
around his waist like a loin cloth

After he ran away from boarding school at age 15
he never again had that dream
in that ending of his prophecy vision
he knew he was the Jesus of Pine Ridge
destined to deliver the full-bloods and half-breeds
to the promised land of the sacred
Black Hills in South Dakota
or at least to the fertile prairie
just south of the state line

into Nebraska or at the very least
anywhere north of Interstate 90

The Jesus of Pine Ridge contemplated
this deliverance into his mid-20s
with a thousand communions of fry bread
and Gibson White Port wine
he figured he needed a sturdy chariot
to lead his people into the promised land
so he bought a car at the reservation border town
of Gordon, Nebraska
traded for a mighty steed
of faded yellow and rust
a 1964 Chrysler Newport
for 260 bucks and 100 dollars in food stamps
the white guy that sold it to him
was some kind of pastor nut
when the deal was done
the white guy laid his hands on the front hood
and preached

"By the power invested in me
in the name of Jesus Christ
I cast the demons and Lucifer
out and away from this vehicle
why just the other day
I laid my hands on a roadkill dog
and brought it back to life"

The Jesus of Pine Ridge knew he was a false God
full of dog doo-doo
tore out of his parking lot

gravel flying like angels in a holy cloud of dust
ripping the plastic Jesus off the dashboard
throwing it in the back seat
laughing and beelining it to the closest liquor store
every car needs a name
so he called it his
Jesus Chrysler

ten years and ten used cars later
he survived countless crazy dumb luck adventures
like the time he could fly
yes, the Jesus of Pine Ridge could fly
well, more like fall
off a 300-ft. cliff
in the Black Hills
a gust of wind and lost footing
found him at the bottom of the canyon
he awoke in a hospital bed
with broken ribs, shattered pelvis, shattered leg
and of course the various cuts and bruises

So the Jesus of Pine Ridge can never die
car accidents
fights
jail time
bad booze and drugs
even falling off a 300-ft. cliff
could never kill the Jesus of Pine Ridge

Maybe he died a long time ago
and this life is his resurrection
the chosen one

to deliver all us full-bloods to half-breeds
into salvation
the Jesus of Pine Ridge

This has been the gospel
according to Luke Warm Water

Reservation Casino
(Fetterman's Revenge)

In the 1860s
U.S. Cavalry Captain Fetterman boasted
"Give me 80 soldiers
and I could ride through the Sioux Nation victorious"

In 1992
on South Dakota Public Television
the tribal president
and editor-in-chief of a local Indian newspaper
told how the casino would bring
money for programs, for the elders and the youth
money for better health care
money for better education
and stipend money for all tribal members
we would make money off the white tourists
visiting the Reservation
I laughed out loud so hard
my ribs hurt
they had learned how to tell believable lies
to their own people
must have learned well
from the white treaty negotiators of the 1800s
they also learned to line their pockets

Captain Fetterman boasted
"Give me 80 soldiers
and I could ride through the Sioux Nation victorious"

Drinking free coffee at the Reservation Casino bar
years later and none of those promises had been upheld
a few Indians work as waitstaff and card dealers

wear black dress pants with white ruffle shirts
and red bow ties
stoic and unsmiling
carrying trays and shuffling cards
they look like the black-and-white pictures
of the early 1900s
like Carlisle Indian School
children wearing suits and dresses
hair cut, in front of buildings
no traditional clothing
no long hair, nor native lodges
in those pictures the children are stoic and unsmiling

Captain Fetterman boasted
"Give me 80 soldiers
and I could ride through the Sioux Nation victorious"

Drinking more free coffee
at the Reservation Casino bar
the bartender looks like George Armstrong Custer
he flirts with the waitresses
the Indian waitresses hiss and hide their smiles
at his pick up lines and bad jokes

Looking down at the carpet beneath my stool
the colorful swirled patterns
look like feathered headdresses
I shut my eyes and listen to a chorus
of slot machines
the cacophony of whistles and bells combine
to make the sound
of a woman

singing a distant traditional song
in native tongue
of sorrow and defeat

Captain Fetterman boasted
"Give me 80 soldiers
and I could ride through the Sioux Nation victorious"

Drinking more free coffee
at the Reservation Casino bar
I have to take a leak
as I walk through the casino I notice the patrons
are mostly Indian
as if drinking, drugs, greed, and jealousy
weren't enough vices for Indians
we can now add gambling to the long list
of addictions

I look into my plastic tub of nickels
fish out an Indian Head nickel
leave it on the bar
as an insult to the bartender
who looks like George Armstrong Custer
not because he looks like Custer
but because he tells lousy jokes
I walk back to the Nickel Slots

With coffee in one hand
tub of nickels in the other
the ghost of Captain Fetterman
now seems to be boasting

"Give me 80 slot machines
and I could ride through the Sioux Nation victorious"

*Epilogue—Captain William Judd Fetterman of the U.S.
Cavalry was a Civil War hero and a casualty of the Fetterman
Fight (which was named for him). The battle took place in the
Powder River country of northern Wyoming on December 21,
1866. Lakota, Arapaho, and Cheyenne killed Fetterman and all
the soldiers under his command during the conflict. In earlier
years Fetterman supposedly had boasted, "Give me eighty men
and I can ride through the whole Sioux Nation victorious."
Ironically eighty men were killed during the Fetterman Fight.*

This Is What It Means to Say San Diego, California

She said, "*Come to San Diego*
and let me run my fingers through
your long, luxurious hair"
she even offered to fuck me half
this would be a great thing because
I am half Indian and half white

She offered, "*I will meet you*
halfway in Al-bah-ker-kee"
where the last time we met
which was the first time we met
immediately adoring each other's hair
but, my car won't go that far
I drank up all the bus ticket money
she sent me

She looks like a Botticelli painting
her smile passionate
breasts beautiful
long flowing hair
acres of ass

She drinks Spanish Sangria for lunch
bottles of fine French wine for dinner
a Gauloises cigarette after each meal

She said, "*Come to San Diego*
read aloud the poetry of Bukowski
while I run
my fingers through
the sound of your voice"

Rapid City Wino Lament

Stumbling through Rapid City wine country
brown paper bag
Mad Dog 20/20 for worse than
blurred vision that keeps
poverty out of focus
Wild Irish Rose for that rotgut
ride on the green lizard
The almighty Thunderbird for
the stars, moon, and the
night skies of flight on
winds on wings
on winds on wings
my gilded Phoenix brothers
and sisters that
you crave to see while
under
     the
       Sixth
          Street
bridge

On Indian Time

Remembering big smiles
a little laughter
from my mother
when she would say
with enthusiasm
"Better late than never"
that was 20 years and more ago
before her passing

Eventually understanding the Lakota significance
of her repeated quote

Indian Time is lost on white people
along with those professional Indians
gauging their lives on promptness and a silk tie

A college friend from the Ft. Berthold Rez
always tried to get my goat
telling me aloud within earshot of others
when I strolled into class late
"There he is, late for Indian Time"
rather than hang my head
in embarrassment shame
I held my head high
sticking my chest out proud
acknowledging him with a big smile
followed by a little laughter

That old college crony
got married young
eventually I lost all contact with him
his wife made him graduate medical school

she makes all his decisions
even what silk ties he wears
he never left North Dakota
retribution for being an "On-time Indian"

Me, I took Spring Break
for a couple years at a time
it took 13 years to finally get
my undergraduate degree
an extra year to finish Grad school
didn't get married until I was 38
no children of my own, yet

I was born in the old Bennett-Clarkson Hospital
which was located in west Rapid City
presently that building
contains the psychiatric unit of Regional Hospital

In life's full richness of Lakota belief
I could come full circle
go completely mad and die
in the same building I was born in
perhaps even the same room

No matter how it ends
someway
somehow
I will probably even be late
for my own funeral

About the Authors

TREVINO L. BRINGS PLENTY is a poet and musician who lives, works, and writes in Portland, Oregon. Trevino is an American and Native American; a Lakota Indian born on the Cheyenne River Sioux Reservation, South Dakota. Some of his work explores the American Indian identity in American culture and how it has through genealogical history affected indigenous peoples in the twenty-first century. He writes of urban Indian life; it's his subject.

ADRIAN C. LOUIS was born and raised in Nevada and is an enrolled member of the Lovelock Paiute Tribe. From 1984 to 1997, he taught at Oglala Lakota College on the Pine Ridge Reservation. Since 1999 he has been a professor in the Minnesota State University system. He has written ten books of poems and two works of fiction. His novel *Skins* was produced as a feature film in 2002 and his writing awards include Pushcart Prizes and fellowships from the Bush Foundation, National Endowment for the Arts, and Lila Wallace–Reader's Digest Foundation. His recent collection, *Logorrhea* (Northwestern University Press), was a finalist for the 2006 *Los Angeles Times Book Prizes*.

STEVE PACHECO is Mdewakanton Dakota from the Lower Sioux Indian Community near Morton, Minnesota. This small reservation, located in southwestern Minnesota, is where Steve resides. He works as an academic and guidance counselor/advocate for high school kids from his community. Some of his previous experiences include teaching, working for tribal government, and dealing blackjack at the casino. Visit *www.dakotacamp.com* for more on Steve Pacheco.

The poet known as LUKE WARM WATER was born and raised in Rapid City, South Dakota, and is an Oglala Lakota (Sioux). He has won Poetry Slam competitions from Oregon to Germany. In 2005, he was awarded an Archibald Bush Foundation individual artist fellowship in literature. Recent poetry books include *Iktomi's Uprising* (2007) and *On Indian Time* (2005).

JOEL WATERS, an Oglala Sioux, was born on the Rosebud Reservation and was raised there and on the Pine Ridge Reservation. He is currently attending the University of South Dakota as an English major. His works have appeared in *Red Ink Magazine, Survivorship Quarterly,* and *The Vermillion Literary Project.* His poetry can also be found in the anthologies *Genocide of the Mind: New Native American Writing* (2003) and *Eating Fire, Tasting Blood: Breaking the Great Silence of the American Indian Holocaust* (2006).